COMING HOME TO LOVE

by Marcia Murphy

© Copyright 2014 by Marcia Murphy. All rights reserved.

No part of this publication may be reproduced or distributed in any form, or stored in a database or retrieval system or transmitted in any form or by any means, electronic, mechanical, photocopying, recording, or otherwise without the prior written permission of the author.

Murphy, Marcia, 1946-
   Coming Home to Love

ISBN #978-0-9916577-0-4

First Edition
1   2   3   4   5   6   7   8   9   10

Printed in North America.

Book and Cover Design: Lotus Design, LotusDesign.biz

DEDICATION

This book is dedicated to my guides and teachers from the Unseen realms whose love, assistance and support made it possible for me to successfully complete my healing journey recounted in these pages. I pray that I can express my gratitude by being of service to others for whatever time remains for me on planet Earth.

May I also express my gratitude to some very dear and special people whose love and kindness made difficult days more bearable:

Anne Guthrie, whose door and heart was always open when I had nowhere else to go.

Christina Toell, whose steadfastness in the face of every trouble lent me strength in difficult moments.

LaAuna Lewis, Brenda Dyer and Michael Martinez, whose compassionate caring saw me through the darkest moments in the early part of my process.

Mary Nadler, whose love and encouragement helped me to stay the course when liberating myself from human consciousness seemed the impossible dream.

Chari Kabat, whose love, kindness and humor brings sunshine to every cloudy day.

And thanks to the countless others, too numerous to mention, who shared, listened and genuinely cared.

TABLE OF CONTENTS

A Note to the Reader 2
Introduction 3

Chapter One: My Personal Background 5
Chapter Two: *Healing Environmental Illness From Within:*
   A Condensed Version 9
Chapter Three: The Interim Years — 2001-2004 17
Chapter Four: The Casa de Dom Inacio, Abadiania, Brazil —
   2005-2011 21
Chapter Five 27
Chapter Six 29
Chapter Seven 37
Chapter Eight 39
Chapter Nine 43
Chapter Ten 45
Chapter Eleven 49
Chapter Twelve: Present Day — 2014 51

Final Thoughts for Readers with Health Challenges 55
Resources 59
About the Author 63

A NOTE TO THE READER

Each person's healing journey is unique. All forms of environmental illness can be very challenging and what works for one does not necessarily work for another. The content of these pages is a summary of my experience and is not intended in any way to be medical advice or to take the place of care by a physician. It is the responsibility of the reader to validate any treatment undertaken with a physician.

I have chosen to share my personal path in this book, realizing that it will bring a variety of responses from readers. Parts of my story may sound like a fairy tale to some people, making it difficult for them to accept the ideas presented. If this describes you, know that I understand your response. Others will resonate with the story, hopefully find it helpful, and benefit in some way. I can only tell you that everything I've written is true and factual and I encourage you, the reader, to take from it what you will that is positive and leave the rest.

INTRODUCTION

It was a proud and gratifying moment in the summer of 2003 when the first copy of my newly published book, *Healing Environmental Illness From Within*, arrived in the mail. As I stood gazing at the cover, the eight long years it had taken to write flooded back into my memory, the many times the writing had been interrupted by bouts of sickness as I struggled with one of the most challenging illnesses of this century—a sensitivity to chemicals and electromagnetic radiation.

As I was enjoying an unprecedented degree of wellness at the time, I believed the book to be a complete story of the healing process I had followed to overcome my illness. There was no way to know I was experiencing only a temporary reprieve in my process or that the *true* cause of my illness had yet to be revealed.

Less than a year later I moved from Boulder, Colorado to Taos, New Mexico and my health took an unexpected turn for the worse. I found myself housebound with what appeared to be reactiveness to the vegetation in my new location. The tools I had used successfully in the past to alleviate such situations were not helpful. I consulted with local doctors, but they had little to offer but the usual supplements and the promise "Next year will be better when your body adjusts to its new surroundings here in New Mexico."

This was my twentieth year with fragile health and by now I knew enough to suspect the root cause of the latest downturn. Desiring wellness above all else, I chose instead to travel to a healing center many miles from my home to address it. Soon another story began unfolding, one that begs to be told in these days when so many people are suffering with chronic illness of all kinds, some still searching for relief when modern medicine has nothing more to offer.

For those of you who don't know me from my first book, a condensed version of that story and my personal background in the next chapter will enable you to understand what I was helped to heal.

CHAPTER ONE
MY PERSONAL BACKGROUND

I was born into a loving family in Boston at the end of World War II. My father had died in the war and my widowed mother worked to support the two of us plus her own mother who lived with us. My mother's younger sister and her husband also lived with us for the first five years of my life, their loving presence making a significant contribution to my early years. My pre-school years were happy ones, marred only by one troubling incident I can still remember as if it were yesterday.

One day when I was four years old I noticed that my mother was not responding to me with the exuberant affection of other family members and I wondered why. I recalled that this had happened before, and when I thought about it I couldn't ever remember hearing her say she loved me. "She doesn't love me as much as the others," I thought. "What could be wrong (with me)?" This thought set the stage for the birth of at least one new belief that would color my world gray from time to time and follow me into adulthood.

As I grew older this observation of my mother repeated itself, and I often noticed her reluctance to speak when her reaction to someone or something was negative. My mother simply wasn't as adept as the others at expressing her feelings, but as a child I didn't understand it and took it personally.

At the age of five, I entered grammar school and reacted unfavorably from the first day of school. I was frightened by the other children and the teachers (nuns) and soon became what was commonly referred to then as a nervous child. Quite simply, I had moved from a world of love into a world of fear and my body responded with frequent periods of sickness, everything from sore throats to digestive upsets. A pattern was set which would follow me into adulthood.

An outsider observing my childhood and young adulthood would probably have described them as ordinary and uneventful. But the people around me did not realize the fear born on the first day of school remained with me on some level all the years of my formal education. As a child I believed I would get over my so-called nervousness, but the only thing that changed as I grew older were my coping skills—I became adept at appearing happy to people around me whenever I was uncomfortable. I thought of it as 'putting on a good face.' But one is never quite happy with a current of fear running just beneath the surface.

My mother and aunt were my primary role models. As a child I idolized the adults in my life and believed they could do no wrong. So it followed that everything they did was worthy of imitation. In many ways my aunt was more like a mother to me as we spent a lot of time together while my own mother was at work. I knew she thought of me as her own child and I loved her dearly, knowing I could always count on her and my uncle to be there if I had a need.

My aunt was a third born child and she saw herself as her mother's 'unwanted one.' She grew up with feelings of rejection and became a people pleaser and rescuer. She demonstrated to me that other people's wants and needs were more important than my own. Being a 'good person' was paramount and in order to be one I needed to put others before myself. In effect, I grew up seeing myself as 'less than' others and my self esteem was always low.

My mother and aunt were good women who always did their best for me. What I couldn't know as a child is that each was coming from a place of woundedness as a result of her life experience with parents and other significant adults. Some children have the ability to avoid taking on what is taught them by their family tribe, so to speak, but I was not one of them, having far too sensitive a nature. So in short you might say I got caught in 'false facts' about myself and the way life is supposed to be.

There is another significant aspect of my childhood upbringing I would like to share with you so you may understand how I was assisted with the spiritual issues contributing to my illness.

I was raised in the Catholic faith and as a child I was very religious, attending church more frequently than most children of my acquaintance. I never doubted for a minute anything I had been taught or had read about my religion, but accepted all on blind faith. I continued in my devotion until, at the age of 21, I became disillusioned with the church and turned away from it as a result of two very distressing incidents in my personal life. Since I saw God and the church as one and the same, I also let God slip out of my life to some degree. You might say I threw the baby out with the bath water.

As the years passed, my conversations with God became less frequent and often took place during periods of my life when I felt desperately in need of help and saw Him as my only recourse. When a trouble passed, I gave thanks to Him for my deliverance from it and went on my way until the next challenge brought me running back to pray earnestly once again. I didn't like my way of relating to God and felt frequent guilt. I wanted a more intimate relationship with Him such as I had enjoyed as a child, but didn't believe I could have it without embracing the church again. I felt powerless to resolve this dilemma for a long time.

If you were to ask me now how I envisioned God as a child and young adult, I would say that I saw Him as somehow situated way above me on a distantly far horizon. I saw myself as small and insignificant, living in the shadow of a great force that had the whole world to watch over, a very big job indeed. I believed He loved me because I had been taught He did, but I never *felt* any love. And because I had also been taught that if I were not 'good,' God would be displeased and I would merit punishment according to how 'bad' I had been, I developed a fear of God.

In other words, I saw God's love as conditional, based on my 'state of grace' at any given time. I saw him as vengeful, promising hell fire to those who did not keep His Commandments. Needless to say, my religious upbringing was a source of much fear.

Upon graduating from high school I accepted a secretarial position offered by a major insurance company in Boston. I worked for the company for 17 years, the first ten in an older office building. Then the company constructed and moved into a new building, complete with brand new carpet, paint, furnishings, and windows that did not open, where I worked as an Executive secretary for seven years. While my job was often stressful, I was a happy, valued employee who enjoyed reasonably good health throughout my years of employment.

In my early twenties I developed a love of nature and the outdoors, spending many happy hours hiking, biking, and skiing in the New England countryside. It was this love of the outdoors and traveling to new places which motivated me to spend my annual two week summer vacation exploring National Parks of the western United States, and eventually led to my decision in 1980 to move to Colorado to be closer to the Rocky Mountains I had come to love.

CHAPTER TWO

HEALING ENVIRONMENTAL ILLNESS FROM WITHIN

A CONDENSED VERSION

In 1981 I moved from my native New England home to Boulder, Colorado and accepted a secretarial position at a major university. For nine years I worked in several positions requiring long hours in front of a computer or standing in front of a copier. During this time I lived in three houses in various stages of remodel—new carpet, paint, and stain. Not recognizing the health dangers it posed, I had an electric blanket on my bed. All this set the stage for an illness of major proportions to develop.

After two years on the job, a series of baffling, seemingly unrelated, symptoms appeared. My eyes began to burn and sting, causing such fatigue I often fell asleep during my morning break. I sought the opinion of one eye doctor after another, but no one could find anything wrong with my eyes. Finally, a specialist discovered a focusing problem and suggested a series of eye exercises which brought some relief, but it didn't eliminate the problem completely.

As time passed, other symptoms appeared: moderate to severe digestive disturbances, bladder pain, and frequency of urination, hypoglycemia attacks, irregular heartbeat, sensitivities to pollens and foods. All this was accompanied by varying degrees of fatigue, requiring bed rest and curtailing all activity outside daily employment at the University. Finally, my health deteriorated to such a degree, I left the University after 6 ½ years of employment.

After six months at home with rest and a complete change of routine I felt well enough to work again and took a part time job as a medical receptionist. While I enjoyed the work, I couldn't support myself on the salary so when the opportunity presented itself to return to the University,

I accepted it. Within the year my health began another slow decline with a variety of symptoms, both old and new, manifesting.

Then one day in 1993 my chiropractor obtained a new piece of testing equipment for his office which allowed him to make an accurate diagnosis of electromagnetic poisoning, a form of environmental illness. By that time my eyes were causing serious concern as all I could read comfortably was the large headline on the front page of a newspaper. My irregular heartbeat was almost off the charts. The doctor, who helped me locate the sources of irritation in both my home and office, refrained from suggesting I leave my job. But it was apparent to both of us that it was a serious threat to my health, and within a week of diagnosis I made the decision to join the ranks of the unemployed for a second time.

After another period of time off and rest, I attempted part-time work in more agreeable settings to support myself and shore up sagging spirits and self esteem, but it did not serve me and my health failed again. Now, in 1995, my chiropractor diagnosed a second form of environmental illness called chemical sensitivity. My body had become reactive to chemical substances found in everyday products such as household cleaners, carpets, furniture, personal care products, petroleum products, etc.

Following this diagnosis my life became challenged beyond belief. I discovered that my workplace was not the only source of environmental stress; my home was a major contributor as well. The indoor air quality of the condo I owned was compromised by chemical products used to clean the carpet throughout the unit and there was insulation in the duct work responsible for sending formaldehyde and mold into the air through the heating system. While I attempted to fix the condo's problems, several friends offered me temporary shelter and I moved from one house to another with my necessary possessions in boxes, sometimes sleeping in my tent in a backyard when I became too reactive.

It was during this problematic period that I heard of Dr. Sherry Rogers, a world-renowned expert in the treatment of environmental illness. Desperate for help I traveled to Syracuse, New York in October 1996 to become her patient. On her recommendation I changed my diet to accommodate numerous food allergies, started phenol-free allergy shots for inhalant allergies, took Nystatin for a yeast overgrowth called Candida, and swallowed handfuls of supplements to correct nutritional deficiencies. While I made the best progress under her care, it still wasn't enough to bring more than temporary relief of symptoms.

Eventually in the spring of 1997 I found it necessary to leave Boulder to escape the growing air pollution problem which Dr. Rogers and I attributed to increased breathing problems. I sold my condo and moved to a friend's chemical-free log cabin in a remote valley in the mountains north of Boulder where I began a year long period of isolation in an attempt to avoid toxicity and heal my sensitive body.

Two months after my imposed isolation began, a friend wanting to help came to visit and suggested I search my soul for any unresolved emotional issues which might be having an adverse effect on my immune system. I began to think seriously about an ongoing, unhappy situation with a close relative and I wondered if fear, anxiety, and feelings of rejection I had experienced for years could be contributing to my illness. I feared if this were true and I didn't address the issue, perhaps I might never recover.

I spent the summer pondering this possibility, following Dr. Roger's protocol and giving my immune system time to heal. Then one day in the fall I awoke with a truth I could no longer deny. My body was not going to heal itself if I continued on this current path and I had to address the emotional component.

A few days later I remembered a place in the Berkshires of western Massachusetts called the Option Institute, a non-profit organization assisting those challenged by adversity to find hopeful solutions to their difficulties. I contacted the Institute and was assisted in selecting a month-long program to best fit my situation. Within the week I was granted a generous scholarship to alleviate my financial concerns and allow me to attend.

During the program I learned of the mind-body connection to illness and discovered the missing puzzle piece preventing my recovery. The culprits were the negative emotions, the fear that had been ruling my life for years, the anger and resentment I had been harboring as a result of traumatic life events from childhood.

The troubled relationship with my family member, which I explored in a private mentoring session, was a key component. It was of such magnitude that shortly after I discovered and let go of two beliefs at the heart of my distress, I stopped reacting to personal care products used by other participants in our shared housing.

By the end of the program, it became clear to me that relieving the physical stressors of my immune system was not enough—emotional stressors needed to be addressed as well if I wanted to recover completely.

In January 1988 I returned to the Institute for another month-long program after being granted a second generous scholarship. The added learning of this invaluable session helped me to see the path to follow if I wanted to make a complete recovery.

Eight months later I moved from Colorado to the Berkshires of western Massachusetts to enroll in the Institute's two year mentor training program. When complete, this training would allow me to help others as the Institute had helped me, and while in training I could continue to work on the personal issues that were contributing to decreased immune function and keeping me reactive.

Before I tell you of my own personal experience at the Option Institute, I'd like to give you an overview of the Institute's philosophy and the method they use to assist people experiencing difficulty in their lives.

Simply stated the main purpose of every Option program is to help people create happiness, peace of mind, and clarity in their lives. One of the principles held at the Institute is that our inner experience and quality of life are the result of what we are choosing to believe in each and every situation life presents. Unhappiness is based on a logical system of beliefs which we have chosen for ourselves or adopted from others in order to make sense of unfolding life circumstances. The beliefs that fuel our unhappiness are changeable. When we change our beliefs, we change the thoughts, feelings, and behavior which stem from those beliefs. By choosing to change our limiting beliefs, we can become happier human beings, more available to ourselves in meeting and solving life challenges.

A nonjudgmental attitude prevails—the Option philosophy holds that people who come seeking help do not need to be "fixed", there is no "right" or "wrong" way to be. We are all doing the very best we know to take care of ourselves based on our current beliefs. The lack of judgment of Institute teachers allows people to explore life issues without fear or hesitation, and unconditional love, and acceptance work miracles every day.

The method of self-exploration used at the Option Institute is called the Option Process Dialogue. In a dialogue a facilitator called a mentor works with an individual offering unconditional love and acceptance instead of advice or direction. The mentor asks a series of nondirective, nonjudgmental questions aimed at uncovering the sometimes complex structure of beliefs underlying behavior and fueling discomfort or unhappiness. The premise is that if we can come to understand why we have drawn the conclusions that we have, we can elect to change the beliefs that have defeated or disempowered us, becoming happier and more at ease in our world.

Mentor training was a stimulating and effective process I was privileged to participate in for two years. The formal training consisted of a weekly two-hour class and thought provoking homework assignment designed to help me delve into my beliefs in every area of life. An instructor reviewed it and then several mentoring sessions followed to help me explore the feelings and beliefs I had uncovered. It was a comprehensive process whose worth cannot be overstated.

From the moment I arrived at the Option Institute in the fall of 1998 one incident after another occurred to show me how my thoughts and fearful reactions to life were affecting my body and contributing to illness. At these times I often sensed what I can only describe as an energetic Presence which both puzzled and elated, giving me a strong sense of comfort that I was not alone in whatever trial was presenting in the moment. Some circumstances were quite challenging, resulting in reactions to chemicals and electromagnetic fields as a result of my response to whatever was happening. Then other symptoms began showing up in various parts of my body which demonstrated to me that my thoughts were responsible for far more than I had imagined. The second half of *Healing Environmental Illness From Within* is devoted to detailing a number of the most revealing incidents and how I came to understand and change the beliefs behind these thoughts and reactions which were at the heart of my illness.

As you might imagine, none of this was easy or a quick fix, but it was worth every minute of effort. Slowly but surely, by making different choices, I was able to move from a victim mentality to a place of empowerment, and as I did so, my health improved. After 18 months in the program my reactiveness to chemicals and radiation quieted down with only occasional flare-ups and I was able to reintroduce foods into my diet to which I had been allergic for years.

Here are the primary issues, fear-based ways in which I was living my life, which were major contributors to my illness:

- Feeling rejected by others.
- Feeling responsible for other people's happiness and unhappiness.
- Blaming others for what happened to me and not taking responsibility for everything I created in my own life.
- Putting my wants second, living my life from a 'should' or 'have to' standpoint.
- Wanting/needing to be perfect.
- Taking responsibility for other people's choices rather than allowing them to be responsible for their own wants and needs.
- Self judgment and judgment of others.
- Non-acceptance of my illness or *myself* with the illness.

In essence, these were all ways in which I didn't love and accept myself.

Many people have difficulty understanding what any of these issues have to do with illness, particularly an illness which obviously involves toxic products in today's world. I can only offer an explanation which allowed me to make sense of this phenomenon for myself, based on three years of observing my own experience.

From early childhood I was engaged in numerous ways of thinking, feeling and reacting which were fear-based in nature, fostering a sense of insecurity and low self-esteem which followed me into adulthood. It is well known today that such a way of being in the world is a continual drain on immune system strength. When my weakened immune system combined with a heightened exposure to toxicity in the mid-'80s, the time and conditions were ripe for a major illness to develop and it did.

In March 2000 I became a certified Option mentor which enabled me to work with people in the Institute's programs. For those of you reading this who are not afflicted with environmental illness, I want to share that many program participants arrived suffering from a variety of physical ailments—arthritis, heart disease, cancer, depression, to name a few. On a number of occasions I observed that those who made a concerted, honest effort to explore and change their thinking and beliefs experienced improvements in their health.

What does it take to heal an illness as devastating as environmental illness? Those of us caught in its grip know there is no one treatment that works for everyone, and therein lies the challenge – there's no easy formula to follow assuring our escape. Some people heal themselves through physical means, for example, by making nutritional and environmental changes and find that sufficient.

For me, emerging from the depths of environmental illness was a twofold process. In the beginning I did what most people do who find themselves reacting to chemicals and electromagnetic radiation—I focused on creating a chemical-free home environment and avoiding people and places that I viewed as unsafe. In other words, I endeavored to create safety in my *external* world. This is an important and logical first step, but it provided me with only temporary relief and it didn't suffice to produce long-term healing.

Eventually I learned that I can only find real safety within myself, in my *internal* world, so to speak. Thus it was seeking and finding a *safe place within* which would allow my body to heal. One could call it a spiritual journey moving from the darkness of fear back into the light of love.

CHAPTER THREE
THE INTERIM YEARS
2001-2004

In the spring of 2001 I left the Institute to return to my former home in Colorado. Over the winter I had devised what I believed to be a good plan. There were many people suffering from environmental illness and other serious ailments who were unaware of how their thoughts and beliefs were contributing to their illness and I wanted to share what I had learned with them. I wanted to establish a private mentoring practice in Boulder to help others as the Institute had helped me.

When I left New England my health was the best it had been in years. While I was still chemically sensitive, I had not experienced a significant reaction in a very long time. I considered my illness 'under control' and never doubted it would remain stable given all I had learned and the tools I could employ to help myself if the need arose.

There was no way to know it would be another three years before I discovered additional fear-based beliefs which had not surfaced during my time at the Institute, beliefs that were responsible for repressed feelings and out of balance behavior that would make it next to impossible to carry out my new life plan with any degree of success. But as the saying goes, ignorance is bliss and so with joy in my heart I drove back across country eager to take up life where I had left off three years earlier.

The first surprise was observing how Boulder had grown during my three year absence. Many people had discovered the charms of this agreeable small city and moved there, their automobiles contributing to the air pollution problem which had been a growing concern when I left in 1998. Two weeks after my return I knew in my heart it was not a good place for me, but I lacked the courage to move again and start over in a place where I knew no one.

With great enthusiasm I began to share my Option experience and what I had learned with both old and new friends alike who were happy to listen, but no one expressed interest in exploring their own situation in like manner. Not one to give up easily, I enrolled in a marketing course which I hoped would jump-start my mentoring practice and it was here I was introduced to a Brazilian-American woman named Gloria who was a hands-on healer. I knew nothing about such a modality and had little faith it could help my sensitivities, but Gloria was such a loving human being, I found myself at her house often over the course of the next several months availing myself of her talents.

In addition to her work in the United States, Gloria also led trips to Brazil to see a healer known as John of God. During our visits she shared stories of the healings she had witnessed, videos of his work, and pictures of people who had been helped at his center. But it wasn't until she suggested I read *Spiritual Alliances* by Emma Bragdon that I realized something extraordinary was happening in this small town in central Brazil. While I wasn't ready to commit to a trip of this nature, I felt drawn to read Emma's book often and always felt unusually energized each time I did so.

The mentoring practice I had envisioned never came to fruition but I used my skills to help whenever I could and limped along through life for almost a year, neither as sick as I had been nor as well as I knew I could be. In the spring of 2003, in an effort to enhance my health, I had the remaining mercury fillings removed from my teeth. While I had an excellent dentist, the process left me drained and ill and removed any remaining doubt the toll this toxic substance had taken on my body through the years. Unable to care for my basic needs, I went to a retreat center in Pennsylvania for a few weeks of rest and rejuvenation and ended up staying seven months while a Canadian doctor who specialized in the process assisted me to detox from the effects of stored heavy metals.

At the end of this period I decided to move to Taos, New Mexico to escape the air pollution in Boulder. Once again, I drove across the country with hope in my heart that my health problems were behind me.

In the spring of 2004, I found a wonderful apartment in Taos to call home. Soon after I moved in, however, two unpleasant incidents occurred resulting in feelings of disappointment and anger which I felt powerless to move past. My sensitivities resurfaced with a vengeance. I sought the help of local doctors who had nothing to suggest but supplements and time.

One morning in June I awoke with a feeling of despair. As I stood in my kitchen on that fateful day, I will never know if the words I heard were my own thoughts or if they came from a source outside myself, "It's time to go to John of God."

CHAPTER FOUR

THE CASA DE DOM INACIO ABADIANIA, BRAZIL 2004-2011

In the highlands of northern Brazil lies a small town called Abadiania (pronounced A-ba-jian-ya). You will not find it on every map, but people from all over the world find their way there nonetheless. Tucked away on a hillside overlooking the beautiful countryside of this region lies a healing center called the Casa de Dom Inacio. It is here that Joao Teixeira, a humble Brazilian man people affectionately call John of God, has been doing his healing work for over twenty-five years.

Joao Teixeira was only sixteen years old when he learned that he was an unconscious medium and that he had the ability to act as a channel of communication between our Earth world and the world of Spirit. At this tender age he committed himself to serving mankind by cooperating with what would become more than thirty non-physical benevolent Beings, allowing them to use his body to perform miraculous healings, both physical and spiritual. In Brazil these Beings are called "Entities" and for the purpose of this story, I will use that word to describe the embodied Beings who work through John of God. These Entities were once revered doctors, surgeons, saints, and noted spiritual men and women in their lifetimes on Earth. As an unconscious medium, Joao has no memory of what happens when the Entity is present in his body.

In the early years, Joao traveled from town to town in vagabond fashion doing his chosen work and for his efforts he was often beaten, abused, and then jailed or run out of town by people who didn't believe his work to be authentic or felt threatened by him. Dedicated to his mission of healing the sick, he persevered through the years of hardship. Then, twenty-five years ago he received assistance to establish his Abadiania healing center. It is called the Casa de Dom Inacio (the house of St. Ignatius) or simply The Casa.

Today the man known as John of God is considered to be the most powerful spiritual healer alive and people come by the thousands from all over the world seeking his help. Through him people have been healed from countless illnesses such as cancer, AIDS, paralysis, blindness, to name just a few. For some people the healing is immediate, but for most, it unfolds over time and requires more than one visit to his center. While belief is certainly helpful, it is not absolutely necessary; many non-believers have received healing in Abadiania and become believers as a result. Conventional and alternative doctors alike have visited and witnessed his work, acknowledging if not fully understanding it.

A trip to John of God's center can be described as a personal healing journey. His work is a reminder of our own ability to connect with the spiritual realms. People of all faiths are welcome and his work is free of charge.

For those wishing to know more about Joao's remarkable life, Robert Pellegrino has written his very moving story in the book *The Miracle Man*.

As I had never been to South America and did not speak Portuguese, I made my first trip to Brazil in July 2004 with an experienced guide named Heather Cumming. I flew from Denver to Sao Paulo, Brazil and then on to Brasilia where I met Heather and sixteen other Americans on her tour. We boarded the bus for the 90 minute ride to Abadiania, and after the long journey I was content to just sit back in silence and enjoy my first glimpse of the Brazilian countryside. I will never forget the beauty of the sky that first evening with the sun peeping through the huge, fluffy clouds, making shadowy vistas on the landscape of the green rolling hills.

We arrived and settled into our room at the Villa Verde hotel which was simple, but comfortable, and then enjoyed a wonderful meal served buffet style in the dining room. The food was cooked to perfection and included beans, rice, chicken, beef, many vegetables, salad items, and an irresistible pudding-like dessert which turned out to be the specialty of the house.

After breakfast the following morning we took the ten minute walk to the Casa for an orientation tour with Heather. I was delighted with the town of Abadiania which is a cross between our modern world and a less developed one. Cars and trucks share the road with an occasional horse drawn wagon, smiling children ride bicycles without gears, chickens and horses cross the street at will, all of it somehow feels so natural and right. It was a typical winter's day, sunny and cool in the morning, weather that stayed with us the entire two weeks.

Arriving on the Casa grounds I noticed a feeling of peace replacing my earlier excitement, a feeling which grew as Heather walked us through the various rooms we would be spending time in the next two weeks. One of these rooms contained discarded crutches and wheelchairs left behind by people who had been cured of their infirmities. As I sat on a bench listening to Heather talk about what we might expect the next day when the Casa opened, I was surprised to experience my peaceful feeling elevating to something close to bliss which remained with me for the entire time we were on the Casa grounds that first day.

Back at the hotel that afternoon each of us met with Heather to review what we had come to Abadiania hoping to heal or experience. I told Heather I was requesting spiritual healing of the root causes of my environmental illness and I handed her a list of what I believed to be my most troublesome issues. Heather suggested I simply ask for healing of the chemical and electromagnetic sensitivities and leave it to John of God's Entities to know what needed to be done to achieve this end. I found myself content with this plan and was blessed with a knowing that whatever I needed would be given to me.

The following day I joined hundreds of other people in the first-timers line to pass in front of the Entity incorporated in Joao, accompanied by Heather who would translate for him what I was requesting. The line passed through two rooms (called Current rooms) where many people dressed all in white sat in meditation with their eyes closed. Heather had explained that thousands of Spirits were at work in both Current rooms cleansing people passing through in the line to see the Entity as well as helping the meditators with their healing process. I was astonished to feel the pulsating energy and never doubted for a moment the presence of unseen forces. When I passed into the second Current room my emotions came to the surface and I felt a strong urge to cry, a feeling that would be re-visited on many similar occasions.

As Heather and I approached the Entity, I saw his eyes take in my body from head to toe. It is said that the Entity reads a person's 'blueprint' instantly and knows what they need on all levels, physically, emotionally, and spiritually. I had never seen a medium in full trance but as I looked at the man known as John of God, I knew immediately that a non-physical Being was in his body. Startled, I dropped to my knees and staring up into the eyes of the Entity, I felt his compassion, kindness, and love. The experience was so overwhelming I have no memory of his words which Heather related to me a few minutes later: "I will heal you, it will require four visits, and you will have invisible surgery this afternoon."

That afternoon seven people in my group returned to the Casa for invisible surgery. Invisible operations are those that occur internally without any external sign of entry into the body and often subsequent x-rays will show an internal incision and sutures. I sat on a bench with others in the room and was told to close my eyes and keep them closed until the surgery was complete. I was told to put my right hand over the area of my body I most wanted to heal; I placed my hand over my heart indicating I most wanted spiritual healing of whatever was causing my physical illness. The volunteer in the room said a prayer and the voice of the Entity spoke briefly in Portuguese.

After about fifteen minutes I was told it was complete and I could open my eyes and exit the room. I walked outside feeling a bit dazed with a moderate fatigue spreading through my body. Heather put the seven of us in taxis and sent us back to the hotel with the firm admonition to spend the rest of the afternoon in bed.

Dinner that evening was a brief, quiet affair. I, for one, needed no encouragement to return to bed until morning as the fatigue of the afternoon had increased considerably.

Thus ended my eventful first day at the Casa de Dom Inacio.

It is customary for everyone who has invisible surgery to go before the Entity in a week's time so he can determine if any revisions need to be made.

Heather accompanied us for this event on Wednesday of the second week when the Casa re-opened. I was directed into the proper room for a short stay of five minutes while a prayer was said and then I spent the rest of the afternoon back in the Current room.

During the rest of my stay I sat in both the first and second Current rooms for my spiritual healing, an integral part of the work at the Casa.

On Friday of the second week when it was time to make the final trip through the line to say thank you and goodbye to the Entity, Heather walked beside me and asked quietly what I wanted to say in parting. "Tell him I will be back before the end of the year for my healing," I replied. As Heather spoke my message to him in Portuguese, the Entity raised his head and graced me with a loving, kindly smile I will always remember. Slowly, the hand in his lap opened inviting me to put mine in his and I was thrilled to feel this special love one last time. In a second it was over and Heather was whisking me away and out the door to join the others in the group who had gone before me.

This last afternoon when the session ended, Joao came outside to greet us as is his custom with Heather's groups. I, for one, found it a thrill to meet the man called John of God, minus the presence of a Spirit. His face is so kind, his humility so evident and speaking only Portuguese he stood silently with each of us while we took pictures. As I stood in his presence, my fatigue disappeared. It was the perfect ending to a challenging, but inspiring, week.

Before I left Brazil, Heather reminded me that although I could not observe external evidence of my surgery, I had received a real operation and care needed to be exercised after I returned home for the remainder of a forty day period. "Absolutely no heavy lifting and lots of rest," she cautioned time and again. Although I intended to comply with the rules, I did not understand the significance of what had transpired. I wondered how I might benefit from the surgery given that environmental illness stresses many areas of the body.

I flew home to Denver expecting to spend the first night with friends and then be on my way to Taos the next morning. But my fatigue was so great I spent the better part of the next three days in bed, accepting the generous offer of my friends to stay with them. I might have been disconcerted with my weakness had my spirit not been enveloped in a most wonderful state of peace for the majority of each day.

On the fourth morning I felt well enough to travel and began the six-hour drive back to New Mexico. I had only been on the road for an hour when I felt an Energy reminiscent of what I had experienced in Abadiania fill the car's interior and I knew that I wasn't alone. An overwhelming feeling of joy filled my heart, waning and then replenishing again, during the entire drive to Taos.

In the weeks following my homecoming I enjoyed significant improvement in the functioning of my elimination and digestive systems, two areas that have been problematic for years. The inhalant allergies that kept me housebound before the trip were absent and never returned. The third blessing I can only describe in this way—it felt like someone had turned down the volume on my nervous system. I walked through my days with an inner stillness I had not experienced in a long, long time. Each morning as I began my day I was aware of an energetic presence surrounding me and as the hours passed I relished periods of intense joy, an emotion that had been noticeably absent for many years. The anger I had been so aware of before the trip was gone and I wondered why I had felt it in the first place.

Prior to the trip, I had been living with a scarcity consciousness and it was more than financial—I felt poor in spirit as I struggled daily with health concerns I couldn't accept. In time I learned that acceptance of what is in my life was the way to inner peace and I could be happy no matter what life handed me if I wanted to, but that lesson was far down the road in July 2004.

CHAPTER FIVE

So eager was I for my healing I returned to the Casa three times in the year following my first trip. On each occasion I received at least one invisible surgery to aid physical healing.

During the first week of my second trip it became apparent that my eyes had been the object of one such procedure. I wasn't aware my vision needed help so I was a bit perplexed at first. I had worn bifocal glasses most of my life to correct both my distance and close vision. When the glasses became impossible to tolerate, I removed them for the rest of the trip. I knew my eyes had been adversely affected by the electromagnetic sensitivity; still, I wondered what the surgery was correcting.

Then one day, without warning, during the last week of the trip my close vision cleared. At this precise moment two tiny insects landed on my arm and to my amazement, I could see the detailed body parts of each with a precision I had never experienced. I spent my last days of the trip staring at every small object in my range of vision and expressing gratitude for the great unexpected gift I had been given by these beautiful Beings. In present day I continue to read without the aid of glasses although my distance vision still requires help.

CHAPTER SIX

During my third and fourth trips many incidents occurred to show me the spiritual root causes of my illness. Whenever people ask me about my experience at John of God's healing center, this is invariably what they ask: "Tell me about the spiritual issues contributing to your illness and how you were helped. What did you learn from it?

The process was twofold. First, I took advantage of every minute I wasn't passing in front of John of God to sit in the Current rooms where I could feel the energy of thousands of helping Spirits at work. Invaluable insights about what I needed to address to bring wellness came to me while sitting in meditation. Second, as I walked through my days, I paid attention to incidents which occurred to show me where my weaknesses and vulnerabilities lay, the areas of my life where I was reacting in a fearful rather than a loving way toward myself and others. Once I saw what I wanted to change in myself, I asked the Entity for help directly or I wrote my thoughts and requests on paper and left it in the prayer basket in the Casa's main hall. In this special place I never doubted the great love at work. I believed that an answer would come in due time and I was never disappointed.

When I arrived in Abadiania in July 2004 I thought I had discovered everything of a spiritual nature contributing to my illness. In truth, I had only scratched the surface. At the heart of my challenges were several undiscovered core issues with attendant beliefs waiting for someone to shine a light so I could see it.

To relate what I learned in a few sentences and without concrete examples is not possible. So, in the following pages I've chosen to share with you some very personal experiences which led me to new conclusions about the root cause of my illness and all illnesses.

During my third trip to the Casa I decided to ask for help with two issues that had been troubling me for some time. The primary one could be described as a deep sense of aloneness which I have felt off and on my entire life. In my younger days I confused it with loneliness and tried to eliminate it by keeping busy with activities. And then for many years I was sure it was the absence of people—sometimes friends and later, a husband. In time I came to know that none of this could fill the void. The emptiness was inside me. It was the absence of love, but whose love? My own? God's?

I believed I would never achieve inner peace if I didn't determine the source of this unwanted feeling and address it. And, not surprisingly, this belief led me to fear the future. Also, after twenty years of illness I had a tremendous need to know that the years ahead would once again hold quality relationships and meaningful work, but, of course, no one could assure me of a brighter future.

I decided to ask the Entity for help to stop fearing my future and secondly, I wanted to experience love in my life and didn't believe I could manifest it for myself. I knew he could see what was in my heart and that he would know what I needed.

In the week following my request I emerged from the Current room one morning and noticed an improvement in my distance vision. Thinking back to the gift of my perfect close vision from the previous trip, I was enjoying a heightened sense of wellbeing. Suddenly it occurred to me that if God, via these beautiful non-physical Beings, intended to give me this great gift of improving my eyesight, it could mean only one thing—He must love me very much! This thought not only startled me, it allowed me to recognize a belief I was holding: "I don't believe God loves me now," I thought, "I need evidence before I believe it." A great sadness threatened to replace the happiness I had been feeling, so I pushed this discomforting subject to the back of my mind for another time.

But the incident soon re-surfaced, refusing to be ignored. One morning I gave it my undivided attention and came to some new conclusions. In fact, I *did* know I was loved, but the knowing was intellectual in nature. I didn't *feel* God's love in my heart. "If I don't feel His Love, do I feel anyone's?" I asked myself. Then I wondered if my inability to feel love, especially God's love, could be the source of this aloneness which had been part of me for so long.

When I passed before John of God the following week, this is what I said: "God loves me, but I don't feel his love. I don't feel my own love for God or myself. Please help me to end this separation between God and me."

The Entity replied simply, "I will help with that."

I don't know what I expected would happen in reply to such a question, but it wasn't mine to worry about. The ball was in the Entity's court.

The following day I sat in the Current room all day and then went back to my room to rest before meeting friends in town for dinner. An hour later I rose to ready myself for the evening ahead. Standing in the bathroom doorway I was thinking about how wonderful a hot shower was going to feel when I heard a voice speaking to me in my mind, quietly, but very distinctly: *"This shower water is my love for you."* As I turned back into the bedroom the communication continued: *"This room is my love for you; this trip is my love for you; the people are my love for you. Feel my love."*

As the words ended, I was standing at the bedroom window staring unseeingly with the full impact of the words washing through me. I had a momentary feeling of shame as I realized how much I had taken for granted lately, especially this trip, but it was short-lived as other realizations followed quickly. The words I had heard held no judgment, only a great love; it was just a reminder of what I had forgotten.

'So, feeling God's love means cultivating a grateful heart,' I thought. Somewhere along the way I had lost the capacity I once had to be truly grateful and it didn't take long to determine why. In the next moments, the recent years of my illness flashed before me. I saw myself giving up one loved activity after another as my sensitivities increased. I saw people, friendships falling by the wayside as I lost the ability to move freely in my world; many days quality of life felt like a thing of the past which might not return. As a result, I began to concentrate only on what I didn't have, rather than appreciating the good in my life that remained.

As minutes ticked by, I was able to observe all this without judging myself. No blame, no hurt, just a simple observing of what had been. But now, I thought, I can change my way of being and return to a place of appreciation for all that has been given to me by God, who loved me enough tonight to remind me of what I've forgotten so that I can heal.

Within the hour I left the room to walk to the restaurant, taking a quiet dirt road paralleling the main street. As I walked, I noticed a number of moving objects: a boy riding toward me on a bicycle with a dog running behind him, chickens pecking in the grass, trees blowing sideways in the wind, to name a few. Without warning, the entire scene before my eyes came to an abrupt standstill while I stood gaping in amazement at some of the objects suspended in air where they were positioned when movement ceased. Then the motion resumed as quickly and easily as it had stopped.

Before I could catch my breath and draw a conclusion, the horse in a field to my left began to shimmer, taking on the appearance of a mirage like a scene in a movie. 'It isn't real, this entire world that seems so solid isn't real; it's simply energy being held in place by a very powerful force,' I thought. Then suddenly the horse returned to its former appearance and I found myself staring at a very solid animal that was now gazing at me with such a tender look of love it brought tears to my eyes.

Eventually the moment ended and I continued down the street and now witnessed this same Love emanating from the trees and flowers, anything I looked at in my path. I was seeing and feeling it all as Love! For the first time, I truly understood the meaning of what I had read numerous times: "Everything is God and God is Love." I had been given the gift of living these words on this walk. Arriving at the restaurant in my altered state, I saw this same light of Love shining in the faces of my friends. It was truly a magical night which I feel at a loss to describe more fully in words.

Before I fell asleep I remembered to express gratitude for the great blessings that had been bestowed upon me in answer to my request to feel God's love.

Friday night was a preview of coming attractions. Walking to breakfast the next morning I experienced the same phenomenon with one difference— I saw and felt this all-encompassing Love with heightened senses which made the experience even richer. It left no doubt that this earth world is not what it appears to be and impressed upon me how much I had to be grateful for in my life.

For the next three days a debilitating fatigue returned making bed rest a necessity, but it was a perfect opportunity to think about the meaning of what I had witnessed. I knew in my heart that this great Love I had been blessed to feel was the God I had wandered away from in early adulthood as a result of upsetting church experiences. This incredible experience was a reminder to me of His existence and how much He still loved me. I also saw it as an invitation to return to His presence and Love, but at this particular time I didn't know how to mend the tear in the fabric of my relationship with God. All I could do was relive the memory, speak to Him in my mind and give thanks for the great gift I had been given.

When this incident occurred only a week of my trip remained and before I knew it, it was time to go before John of God to bid farewell which is customary before one leaves his healing center. When I approached the Entity I was holding a paper in my hand with two items on it: a statement of thanks for all the help I had been given and a question: "On my next trip to Abadiania in May, how long would you suggest I plan to stay?" As there was nothing in this question to cause me discomfort, I couldn't understand (then or now) my mounting anxiety or hesitation to ask it as I moved forward in line.

At the last minute I found myself folding the paper before handing it to the translator so he read only the first part. The Entity listened, then seconds ticked by before he replied which is unusual. Eventually he said, "OK dear." It was only later I realized he knew there was a question I hadn't asked and I can only surmise he may have been giving me the opportunity to do so. The minute I left the Entity's presence I began to feel exceedingly uncomfortable, almost the way a child does after he's tried to deceive a parent. But I was so caught up in wondering about the reason for my omission and regretting I didn't have an answer, I didn't recognize the true source of my discomfort.

By the time I met friends for dinner that night, a sore throat had developed and I was feeling sick all over. I hardly slept that night. The next morning my sore throat was worse and both ears were blocked. I was flying home within 48 hours and knew it wasn't wise to fly with blocked ears, nor did I feel capable of traveling for two days without sleep. But the physical symptoms were mild compared to the angst I felt remembering the previous afternoon's incident.

Thinking along these unhappy lines, I began to pace the room reliving the events of the previous afternoon when I heard the Entities communicating with me in my mind: *"The issue is not the content of the question, the issue here is you not loving yourself enough when things like this happen."* I heard no judgment in the words, only an explanation so I could see the situation in its true light. And the light dawned all right—I realized how caught up I had been in self-judgment and that was the source of the turmoil and the physical sickness which had manifested.

To understand the degree of distress I felt in this moment, you would have to know how much effort I have put into moving beyond self-judgment. To calm myself, I left the room and walked to the Casa where I sat on a bench in the gardens and contemplated the events of the morning. As I sat gazing at the beauty all around me, a single voice communicated with me: *"When you judge yourself, you judge Me because there's a part of Me inside you. If you don't judge and you love the people I send you, you will feel your love for Me."*

I remained seated for another fifteen minutes feeling so very loved after hearing these words. And then I proceeded back to my hotel, deciding on the way that the time was not right to leave this special place.

I remained in Abadiania for an additional two weeks. It was an invaluable time as the Entities continued to show me those behaviors I was fixed upon in daily life that didn't serve me and kept me stuck in my pattern of illness.

The next assistance of major proportion came to me in response to a request I made to the Entities while sitting in the Casa gardens the following week. I had been experiencing visual blurring so I asked them to help me see what I needed to see in my life before my vision could clear. I told them I didn't care how emotionally painful it might be, I was willing to face it.

What happened next took the form of a series of thoughts following in rapid succession, and I was aware it was transmitting into my mind from a source outside myself. First came the question: "When is my distance vision going to clear?" Next, I was given to realize how much time I was spending thinking about this subject—my trying to know the timing of a future event only a higher power can know produces a significant drain on my energy level and comes under the heading of trying to control.

Then I was shown the bigger picture – how much time I've spent in my lifetime engaging in this activity of trying to control. Finally, I saw and felt how freeing it would be if I didn't do this any more, if I simply lived my life by 'letting go and letting God.' And in the next moment, that is exactly what happened: I felt a tremendous letting go inside, shaking me to the core of my being.

I sat in the garden another fifteen minutes with feelings of relief and joy washing through me as I realized how different my life could be free of the need to control. As control has many faces, I wasn't certain I was finished with it, but I made a silent vow to watch for signs of it, especially after returning home.

CHAPTER SEVEN

When John of God's Entities began taking me through the spiritual healing process in earnest during my third trip to the Casa, these were among the first incidents that occurred to show me prime root causes of my illness. Before I came to Abadiania I did not attribute my lukewarm relationship with the One who created me to have anything to do with the sickness in my body and I would have considered it preposterous if anyone had suggested it to me. These experiences allowed me to see how wonderful my life could be if I chose to open my heart to this God-Love I had wandered from so many years ago.

I would like to tell you that my life altered irrevocably after what I've just described in these pages, but it wasn't quite that dramatic. I was not always able to connect easily and quickly to my Creator in every situation life presented nor was I able to drop judgment of myself immediately. It was a process I had to work on over a period of time. But now my eyes were open to the possibility of a healthier and more joyous life and most importantly, I desired to make an effort toward a closer relationship with this great Love I had distanced myself from. And with my desire to reach out to my Creator, He reached back to me, sharing his Love in unexpected moments and places.

A few days after I returned home from my third trip I went out into the yard to retrieve something from my car when a small bird landed on a nearby fence. As I looked at the bird, I thought, "This bird is my love for you." No voice this time, only my own thought, but the thought was accompanied by a feeling of great love and connection to God, identical to what I had experienced so many times during my last two weeks in Brazil. I walked back in the house feeling such joy which remained with me as I went about my daily chores.

CHAPTER EIGHT

When I returned to the Casa for my fourth trip, another incident added to my new perspective and showed me that a variety of health consequences can result from absence of the Creator's Love.

One day I had the good fortune to meet an Australian woman I'll call Mary who was suffering from terminal cancer. According to her doctors, she had only a few months left to live. Prior to her visit, a friend had brought Mary's picture to John of God requesting help for her. The Entity in Joao's body that day said he would help Mary, but that it would require her presence at the Casa. When she heard this news Mary made arrangements to go in spite of the great difficulty it would entail—she had 24 hour nursing care and was in a wheelchair.

A week after Mary arrived she sent her nurse home to Australia and gave away her wheelchair. She had not received healing of cancer, but she was able to take care of herself again and move around on her own.

Several times a week Joao comes out into the main hall where people are waiting and gives them the opportunity to observe the Entity entering his body. After the incorporation the Entity will often pick people from the crowd to join him on the small stage and help them in some way. One afternoon Mary was selected and, as I was standing nearby, I witnessed her great blessing at close range. Putting both hands on her head, the Entity looked straight into her eyes for about a minute. The dramatic change in Mary's facial expression told me that something monumental was occurring. From that day forward Mary was a different woman radiating peace and joy from the inside out for everyone to see.

Later the same week an opportunity presented itself to spend time with Mary and hear of her experience firsthand. She surprised me with these words: "I thought that God didn't love me, it was the cause of my illness. But when the Entity looked into my eyes, I saw the truth of God's love for me at last."

As I write this, I can still remember how sorry I felt that Mary had suffered so because of her long-held belief. At the time I met Mary I was unaware that I was suffering from a similar illusion due to a belief born in childhood. I know now that Mary was in my path to reflect back to me what was going on within me.

Summing up the spiritual revelations that first year at the Casa, it was a time of not only reconnecting with the Divine, but also a time of coming home to myself. I was shown those areas of my life where I had become out of balance and wasn't loving myself.

Here are some additional ways I related to the world which didn't serve me that I was encouraged to change:

Since childhood I had perceived myself as somehow less than others and in focusing on giving others what they wanted, I often had difficulty determining my own wants. On the surface this might appear simple to remedy, but I wasn't cognizant of my behavior so it took many incidents to bring me to awareness of the happiness and joy I was missing by not considering my wants in a given situation.

I was also shown that when I did want something, I was afraid to ask for it. It was a behavior begun in childhood to avoid the pain of a negative response. I still remember the patience and persistence of the unseen forces at work in the Current rooms (and all over Abadiania for that matter) who whispered encouragement to me to ask, ask, ask. Slowly, but surely, I came to trust that the Entities were waiting and willing to help me if I were willing to ask for it. In time, asking became a time of joy instead of an exercise in fearful imaginings that I would be denied. And eventually the day arrived when I could even drop preferences of how they would answer a request, trusting them to know best what I needed and give it to me.

At every opportunity I was encouraged to follow my heart when making decisions. While logical thought process has its place, I was too much in my head and more often than not, my choices weren't what I truly wanted and resulted in disappointment and self-judgment. Learning to be guided by my heart took practice but the reward of greater happiness is well worth the effort.

Learning to trust was one of my biggest challenges. My life experience, both before and after my illness, had taught me to distrust just about everyone—a loving Source, myself and, of course, other people. At the Casa

I learned through some very intense experiences that not to trust God was to live in a continual state of fear over one thing after another. And I learned that God is waiting to give me what I desire if I simply ask and trust that he will provide it or something better at an appropriate time, His time and not mine, I might add.

And finally, I was helped to see the benefits of feeling all of my feelings. I had become so adept at avoiding the so-called negative ones that I could no longer experience a full measure of the happiness and joy I wanted to feel. It was like living in a gray world where the mediocre is all that is available. And I also learned that the quickest way to pass through pain was to feel it fully rather than attempting to push it away.

CHAPTER NINE

One day toward the end of my fourth trip I passed in front of John of God to announce my intention to leave the following week and ask whether I needed to stay longer for my healing. Before the translator could express these words for me, the Entity told me I would have invisible surgery the following morning.

When I emerged from the invisible surgery room the next morning I paused briefly to wait for a friend. A man walked past me and stopped nearby to take out a cigarette and light it. Cigarette smoke was one of my worst offenders, but on this particular occasion I had no time to move out of the way and the smoke went right in my face. For the first time in twenty years no reaction resulted from inhaling the fumes. "Could it be?" I thought, "Could it be the surgery ended my chemical sensitivity?" But I couldn't allow myself the belief; it seemed too good to be true.

For the next week I went out of my way to expose myself to auto exhaust and any other chemical I could find. I was looking for evidence that my illness was a thing of the past; some part of me still couldn't grasp the idea.

On the seventh day after surgery I went before John of God and the Entity in his body confirmed that my healing was complete and I could go home. It was almost a year to the day I had first appeared before him asking for help and he had kept his promise. I had made four trips to Abadiania and had spent a total of seven months in the healing process.

CHAPTER TEN

My story might have ended with this fourth trip. I could have returned home with my newly healed body and taken up life again free of the complications of chemical sensitivity and forgotten all I had experienced at the Casa. But it wasn't possible as something inside me had been profoundly altered, and I knew I had to return to this healing center when my intuition told me the time was right. Deep inside me I knew that my all important relationship with this One I called God was not healed and I felt there was no better place to get additional help than the Casa.

In early November of that same year it came as no surprise when I awoke one morning with a call to return. I made plans for my fifth trip in January of 2006. I was not aware of any physical challenge in my body requiring attention, but it didn't prevent my feeling gratitude when I received another invisible surgery which corrected a long-term back problem requiring frequent visits to my chiropractor. And once again, I received spiritual blessings making my effort worthwhile.

Since then I have continued to make trips to the Casa once or twice a year and each time I received many blessings of additional physical healing and spiritual help. Of all the incidents which occurred on subsequent trips I would like to share with you the one which, perhaps, had the greatest impact.

While sitting in the Current room one day some discomforting scenes from my childhood began running through my mind like a movie being shown on a screen. The movie portrayed me as a beautiful child full of light dancing through the early years of life when suddenly the light was extinguished leaving only a shadow of the child behind. As I watched, it was clear that the source of the difficulty was my relationship with my mother.

Emerging from the Current room I felt a strong urge to cry, but was not certain why until I reached the Casa gardens and heard a voice speaking to me of a belief I was not aware I was holding: *My mother doesn't love me. If my mother doesn't love me, how could God love me, or other people?*

Hearing these words took me back to a family Sunday when at age four this belief was born, a belief I had never admitted to myself to avoid feeling pain. I was unaware of the second part of the belief about God's love, but now there was no denying it. I knew in my heart the words I had heard were true and in the next moment the significance of it hit home. I had never thought of myself as separated from God, but one who doesn't feel loved by the Source is surely experiencing the illusion of separation. And then I saw it—this was the first cause behind my illness—the situation which needed remedying if I wanted to enjoy a full measure of health and happiness.

Over the next few weeks several more significant incidents occurred to show me how family dynamics had contributed to the decline of my immune system strength. It was a relief to understand why it had been so difficult to let love into my life for years and where the feelings of unworthiness had started. I spent much time in a quiet contemplative state thinking about my family, feeling and releasing grief, and while it wasn't easy, the time was invaluable for the clearing it brought.

After returning home it became apparent that I had a lot of forgiveness work to do, and that was when I realized I knew nothing about the subject of forgiveness. In an effort to educate myself on the subject, I borrowed a DVD from the local Noetic Sciences library featuring Dr. Fred Luskin, Director of the Stanford Forgiveness project and author of *Forgive for Good*. Some of what I heard surprised me and it was so helpful, I have summarized Dr. Luskin's main points to share with you:

- Forgiveness is making peace with your life when you don't get what you want. It means holding soft your life experience when someone treats you unkindly, and whatever the unkindness is, forgiveness means it stops with you.
- Forgiveness is an inner heart cleansing, a reopening to life without the prejudice that comes with it because you were not treated well. And in reopening to life, it is realizing there are some people you are better off without.

- Forgiveness is not reconciliation. If someone has hurt you, forgiveness does not mean you have to welcome them back into your life or re-initiate any relationship unless you want to do so. There is as much forgiveness in saying "I am whole within myself, but you are not welcome here" as in saying "Come on back."

- Forgiveness is not forgetting. How can you forget some of the worst things that have happened to you? You can forgive without forgetting.

- Forgiveness is not condoning bad actions. Many people think forgiveness means making the thing that happened okay and if you make the thing okay, you don't have to forgive. We need to be able to discriminate between what is okay and what isn't okay and to hold the things that are not okay with gentleness and without bitterness, knowing that everyone fails. It also doesn't mean that there are not consequences to pay for people who commit certain offenses.

- Forgiveness is necessary because people fail all the time at being successful in their lives or being good human beings. We live with uncertainty and vulnerability and everything is a risk. It is a dire human need to make peace with our experiences and it is neglected in everyone. We keep our heart open when bad things happen because none of it is going to go away and if we choose not to forgive, we suffer.

In time I came to see how I could apply some of what I heard on the DVD to my family situation and individual family members. I began to view each person as having done the very best they could for me and for themselves. I made it okay to move away from one family member for awhile during my healing process and gave up feeling guilty about it.

Still, I was aware that there was unresolved grief and anger under the surface which needed to be released so I sought the help of a therapist near my home. After working with her for three months, the grief was greatly diminished, but I could not access the anger no matter what she suggested.

What helped most in the end was a reading of the book *Radical Forgiveness* by an Englishman named Colin Tipping who also offered multiple-day forgiveness courses. The book helped me to view my family situation from a spiritual perspective laying the foundation I needed to get the most out of his forgiveness workshop which I completed the following summer.

I found Colin to be a master at helping people explore painful situations from their past and release the internalized anger. Thankfully, his efforts on my behalf were successful, and when my anger came to the surface to be released, forgiveness of family members followed. Forgiving myself was another matter and the grieving process was a lengthy one. Finally, I took Colin's self forgiveness workshop and eventually the wounds resulting from childhood misperceptions healed.

CHAPTER ELEVEN

Since my healing in 2005 I have made eight additional trips to John of God's Casa, sometimes from necessity, but more often for the love and joy it gives me to be there. And each time I have been richly rewarded as the Entities who work through this humble man continue to shower me with numerous blessings in the form of invisible surgery and spiritual help to move beyond what keeps me from being at peace in my life.

A few years ago a most beautiful Being reminded me of what I had forgotten to make a priority in my life: "Spend some time with your Creator each day in whatever way is most meaningful to you," she encouraged me. At first I wasn't sure how to do this. I perceived it meant spending time in lengthy periods of formal meditation which I've never been very good at doing. So I decided to begin by simply talking to the One while walking in nature and then as I went about my daily tasks whenever it came to mind. Conversations increased in frequency and over time a deeper relationship developed until the day arrived when I realized that God had become my best friend. Eventually I came to trust my new friend which allowed me to let go of trying to control everything in my life and freed me to concentrate on loving others.

In essence, it all begins and ends with love—first and foremost loving the Creator and then myself and others. Simple, yet at the same time, profound. In concentrating on sharing my love each day, my reward is peace, happiness, and improved health.

One last sharing for those of you who can't (or don't feel drawn to) go to the Casa, know that it is not really necessary to have experiences such as I have described. God and Love are right here. While I view my time at the Casa as one of my life's highlights, incidents of similar magnitude have occurred to me right here at home. Asking for help and opening one's heart to let love in every day can work miracles.

CHAPTER TWELVE

PRESENT DAY 2014

In 2008 I moved from Taos to Asheville, North Carolina after requesting and receiving guidance at the Casa during my annual trip. This move was instrumental in setting the stage for the next phase of my journey to foster a more meaningful relationship with my Creator.

While attending a spiritual workshop in Asheville two years later, I met a woman named Mary Nadler whose love, happiness and joy were apparent at once. As we became acquainted, I learned that her work was to help people achieve higher consciousness, to move from a state of human consciousness (fear, judgment, blame, anger, resentment, etc.) to one of God consciousness (love, joy, peace, happiness, etc.) For this purpose Mary had nine Ascended Masters working with and through her during her group workshops and private sessions with individuals. I learned that Ascended Masters were souls who had once lived on this Earth in physical bodies as you and I have and who gained mastery on this plane of existence. Residing now in higher dimensions, they devote themselves to helping people on Earth aspiring to follow in their path and achieve Self-Realization.

For those of you who are not familiar with the term Self-Realization, it is described in this way in the book *The Yoga of Jesus* published by the Self-Realization Fellowship founded in 1920 by Ascended Master Yogananda: Self-Realization is "the knowing—in body, mind, and soul—that we are One with the omnipresence of God; that we do not have to pray that it come to us, that we are not merely near it at all times, but that God's omnipresence is our omnipresence; that we are just as much a part of God now as we will ever be. All we have to do is improve our knowing."

I was not familiar with either Ascended Masters or Self-Realization, but my experiences with John of God and the non-physical world of the Casa allowed me to open my mind and heart to this potential new path.

When I met Mary in 2010 I was still making annual trips to John of God's center, and while I felt reasonably happy most days, I was aware of being stuck in human consciousness ways that didn't serve me; some examples would be self-judgment, feelings of unworthiness, or blaming others for what happened to me. I wanted very much to move beyond these ways of being that kept me from loving myself so I could enjoy life to the fullest.

I began attending Mary's workshops and a year later added private sessions. A whole new world opened up, one very different from previous experience and, as I opened my heart to embrace it, life improved as human consciousness ways fell away slowly but surely. Other people with similar wants and needs found their way to Mary's door and gradually we became a committed group of individuals with a common goal of achieving Self-Realization.

In present day I am still a member of this same group with a stronger sense of commitment than ever before. In the past two years new members have joined us and more continue to arrive every month. In addition to attending the workshops which Mary still offers, we meet each Wednesday morning for an hour to receive additional energetic blessings from the Ascended Masters who continue to help us in our evolvement as souls. Our group is not exclusive and we welcome other people who feel drawn to join us.

In the past year our group has been blessed to receive what I would describe as downloads of Divine Light and Love which have been aptly named Living Light Blessings. After receiving many of these beautiful blessings, each of us was initiated into the process of passing them on to other people who feel drawn to receive them. In my humble opinion, this is perhaps my greatest gift as so many in the world today are experiencing some form of pain with no way they can discern to alleviate their suffering. Divine Love, which is the essence of the blessing, is not limited by time or space so it can be passed on to persons at a distance as well as in person.

As I write these concluding words, nine years have passed since my healing on that faraway continent. Now more than ever before, I am aware of the role love plays in healing, not only physical illness in humans, but how crucial it is for the healing of our planet and all mankind. I feel blessed to spend a portion of my remaining Earth years sharing my gifts and abilities with those who want to increase the love quotient in their own life to radiate out to our dear planet.

FINAL THOUGHTS FOR READERS WITH HEALTH CHALLENGES

Practically speaking, I realize there are many people who cannot attend an Option program or go to see John of God in Brazil in an effort to resolve health challenges. But if you find yourself resonating with the story in these pages, know that there are other paths to follow closer to home to help you find your way back to a happy, healthy lifestyle. I would like to offer you some final thoughts for a place to start based on what I've learned along the way and share with you ways in which I might help you if you feel it is appropriate for you.

These are the words of an Ascended Master whose guidance is invaluable to me in my own journey:

If you have a health problem you can go to every doctor in the world, the health food store, a nutritional counselor, do every therapy in the world. If you don't examine the relationship of that illness to the Love in your life or the lack thereof, you're not going to find the answer.

The prime cause is Love.

Before you look for any other cause, look for Love.

If you believe there may be emotional/spiritual issues contributing to your illness, but you don't know what they are, ask yourself these questions:

Where do I feel separated from love? (God's Love, self-love, and love for others.) What keeps me from feeling peace in my life? What contributes to a sense of disharmony as I walk through my days?

Who among us has not had experiences which have effectively stolen our peace and left us feeling separated from love in some way? It's all part of the human condition and no one is exempt. Further, as challenging life events occur, beliefs about ourselves, other people and situations develop, many times slipping beneath the surface of our consciousness where they affect our daily life, how we react to people and events around us.

How might I help you?

For those who can relate to this idea of beliefs, I offer my mentoring skills to assist you in discovering your own disempowering beliefs (we all have them!) at which time you, and you alone, have the choice to change or drop them. During my time working at the Option Institute I witnessed many lives taking a 180 degree turn for the better with the discovery and elimination of a single belief that had been present and operating for years, creating all kinds of angst in the person's heart. Beliefs have the ability to separate us from self-love, God-Love, and love for others.

Once any emotional/spiritual issues have been identified, the next question becomes "What am I willing to do or change in myself to alleviate the body burden these stressors present?" Oftentimes the price we must pay for peace is to change our reaction to whatever life hands us. Sometimes, the only solution is forgiveness.

There are many healing tools available today to assist one in restoring love if it is our intention to do so. I am available as an impartial party to discuss options with people who desire help in this regard.

For readers with environmental illness

I want to mention how important it is to find a doctor you can trust and respect who has been trained to treat this challenging illness. In my first year I went to many doctors who thought their method was effective. And while they offered their best, their treatments fell far short of bringing anything but temporary relief.

My own doctor was Sherry Rogers in Syracuse, N.Y. who has many books available which are listed under Resources. Her very effective protocol was to test for all stressors of the immune system on her patient's first visit and treat them all *simultaneously*. She had environmental illness herself and had learned that to address one stressor at a time did not bring success. I can vouch for the validity of that statement in my own process.

How might I help you?

For those of you who want to speak with someone who truly understands the illness, I might be a good fit to help you explore avenues to pursue for your own healing. I offer a complimentary half hour for anyone wishing to make this determination. I believe that we all have our own answers, but sometimes we need help to access them and an impartial party can be invaluable in this regard.

My offerings for local Asheville people

Several years ago I was given permission to bring home from Brazil what is called a John of God Crystal Bed and I offer sessions in my home for those who feel called to experience it. The Beings of Light who work through John of God also work through the Crystal Bed so I encourage people to set an intention or to ask for help with some physical, emotional or spiritual issue at the beginning of the session.

The Crystal Bed is a unique healing modality used daily at John of God's healing center. There are seven geometrically cut quartz crystals suspended above the bed which align with and correspond to the seven chakras of the human body. The crystals radiate color to the respective chakras to cleanse them and balance their energy. Any energy blocks are effectively removed from the body. Improvement can occur on all levels—physical, emotional, and spiritual. A picture of the Crystal Bed can be viewed on my website (marciaamurphy.com).

A person receiving a session, which takes 45 minutes, lies fully clothed on a massage table with closed eyes, listening to soothing music if desired.

It is suggested to allow an additional 15-20 minutes after the session to sit quietly before resuming daily activity. It is also advisable to drink several glasses of water over the next few hours.

What might one expect to experience?

Persons who choose to have a session report a variety of effects, often varying with each session, unique to his/her own condition and level of awareness. Common reports include:

- Stress relief and a feeling of deep relaxation.
- Feelings of peace, serenity, and overall well being.
- An increase in energy.
- Feelings of physical and/or spiritual healing taking place.

- Insights gained into life situations and the cause of disease states.
- Insights into future life path.
- A deep tiredness (as a result of healing that has occurred).

For some the effects might not present visibly, but will happen on a subtle energetic level. The experience is entirely individual.

As a result of my work with the Ascended Masters in my Self-Realization group, I am initiated to bring in what is called a Living Light Blessing. This blessing could be described as a download of powerful, loving Divine energy to raise the consciousness of the recipient, no matter where he or she is at present. The individual is gifted with whatever is needed in the moment.

I have received many such blessings and each one has been unique—at times I have felt a dramatic rush of energy throughout my body which awakens a feeling of unity with my Creator; at other times the blessing comes in quietly and peacefully and I'm reminded how very much I am loved by the One. Whichever form the blessing takes, it leaves me feeling uplifted, grateful, and in my flow.

There will be as many descriptions of the blessing as there are people to receive. A Living Light blessing must be experienced to be appreciated.

One should allow 20-30 minutes and be in a position to sit or lie down during the session. Living Light blessings can be done just as effectively from a distance (via phone) for people unable to come in person.

I am offering complimentary blessings for an indefinite period so as many as possible can experience this beautiful gift. You can contact me by phone or through my website marciaamurphy.com.

RESOURCES

Tours to John of God

If you will be going to Brazil by yourself for the first time, it is not absolutely necessary to go with a guide, but it is very helpful and I would highly recommend it. On my first trip I went with a guide named Heather Cumming and it was a very positive experience in every way.

You will find a wealth of information for planning a trip to the Casa on this website: friendsofthecasa.com. If you are looking for a tour group, scroll down on the home page of this website until you find "Official Tours to the Casa." Enter the country you will be traveling from and if it's the USA, you will find offerings from many guides. I am familiar with these guides: Josie RavenWing, Heather Cumming, Bob Dinga and Diana Rose. I would recommend any one of them as an excellent choice to accompany you.

Each week an orientation for newcomers is held at the Casa which is a must to attend if you are traveling independently.

Another option to consider

If you are unable to go to the Casa, you can send your picture to John of God with another individual who is willing to take it before him on your behalf. In most instances herbs will be prescribed. The herbs, which come in capsule form, are simply passionflower herb and they will be blessed especially for you to help with your specific situation or request. Taking the herbs is your part in the process. If you are not willing to take them, it is better to ask that your picture be placed in the prayer triangle in the main hall of the Casa. Know that this is a very powerful option. Your picture will still be addressed, but herbs will not be part of the help you receive.

Self-realization groups and information

Information on Mary and Barry Nadler, who head my Self-Realization group, can be found at mastersway.us. There are twelve members in the Asheville, NC area, but it is not necessary to live here to participate in

Mary's workshops or her other offerings. There are individuals in a number of States and Canada who participate long-distance via a conference call line.

There is another Self-Realization group which meets in West Asheville on Sunday morning and Wednesday evening. For information on this group, email ashevillesrf@gmail.com.

For additional information on this subject, you may go to the official website for Self-Realization Fellowship in Los Angeles, CA which is yogananda-srf.org.

The Option Institute
The Institute is located in the Berkshires of western Massachusetts in the town of Sheffield. Their website is option.org and a catalog of their program offerings can be requested by calling 1-800-714-2779. Financial assistance is offered for those who have need of it to attend a program.

Books you might find useful:
Three books written by Sherry A. Rogers, M.D.
The E.I. Syndrome Revised
Tired or Toxic?
Wellness Against All Odds

Healing Environmental Illness From Within by Marcia Murphy
This is my first literary offering which contains more detailed information than the synopsis in this book. In it I describe the development of my illness, my experiences with various medical professionals, what helped and what wasn't useful. For those people who have difficulty understanding the mind-body concept, the second half of the book is devoted to explicit life examples contributing to the illness and how I addressed them to achieve a reprieve from my sensitivities. Some readers have told me that its ultimate message makes it helpful for a wider audience than people with environmental illness. A copy may be obtained by contacting me directly and it's also on Amazon.

Feelings Buried Alive Never Die… by Karol K. Truman
Anything you could think to ask about feelings is covered in this easy to read and understand book—why we feel the way we do, where feelings originate, what to do when feelings have been repressed and more.

Radical Forgiveness by Colin Tipping

The best book I've ever read on the subject of forgiveness. In addition to his book, Colin also offers forgiveness workshops which I found very effective in helping me to forgive others and myself. To see a complete schedule of his offerings, go to colintipping.com. He now has online programs and does live programs in Europe.

ABOUT THE AUTHOR

Marcia currently resides in Swannanoa, a small town bordering Asheville in western North Carolina. She offers sessions on a John of God Crystal Bed in her home for those people interested in availing themselves of all this special modality has to offer. She is also a facilitator of Living Light Blessings which is available in person or over the phone for those at a distance.

When not pursuing spiritual interests, Marcia participates in weekly yoga classes and enjoys hiking in the beautiful Blue Ridge Mountains of North Carolina.

One of her current goals is to spread a hopeful message that environmental illness does not have to be a life sentence, to help people with health challenges to understand the effect of spiritual and emotional stressors on the immune system and the power of Love to bring healing. In line with this goal, Marcia is available to speak about her experience with individuals or small groups of people about any part of her journey. She welcomes questions and comments from readers.

Contact information:
Website: marciaamurphy.com
Email: marciainasheville@gmail.com
Phone: 828-225-1735

www.ingramcontent.com/pod-product-compliance
Lightning Source LLC
Chambersburg PA
CBHW031424040426
42444CB00006B/695